CATS
SET III

Scottish Fold Cats

Julie Murray
ABDO Publishing Company

visit us at
www.abdopub.com

Published by ABDO Publishing Company, 4940 Viking Drive, Edina, Minnesota 55435.
Copyright © 2003 by Abdo Consulting Group, Inc. International copyrights reserved in
all countries. No part of this book may be reproduced in any form without written
permission from the publisher.

Printed in the United States.

Photo Credits: Ron Kimball pp. 7, 9, 17, 21; Animals Animals pp. 10, 11, 15, 19;
   Corbis pp. 5, 13
Contributing Editors: Tamara L. Britton, Kristin Van Cleaf, Stephanie Hedlund
Book Design & Graphics: Neil Klinepier

Library of Congress Cataloging-in-Publication Data

Murray, Julie, 1969-
   Scottish Fold cats / Julie Murray.
      p. cm. -- (Cats. Set III)
   Summary: An introduction to the origins, physical characteristics, and behavior of
Scottish Fold cats, with information on the choosing and care of a Scottish Fold kitten.
   ISBN 1-57765-867-1
   1. Scottish fold cat--Juvenile literature. [1. Scottish fold cat. 2. Cats.] I. Title.

SF449.S35 M87 2002
636.8'22--dc21

                                                         2002016385

Contents

Lions, Tigers, and Cats

The first cats lived about 35 million years ago. There are several different types of cats. They all belong to the animal family **Felidae**. There are 38 different species in this family.

Cats are organized into three different categories. Examples of big cats are lions, tigers, jaguars, and leopards. The small cats include **domestic** cats, lynx, and bobcats. Cheetahs are in a group by themselves.

Domestic cats are believed to be the ancestors of the African wildcat. Cats were tamed about 4,000 years ago in Egypt. Today, there are more than 40 different recognized **breeds** of domestic cats.

Because they are in the same family, this big mountain lion has many of the same characteristics as a Scottish Fold!

Scottish Fold Cats

The first Scottish Fold was discovered in Pertshire, Scotland. In 1961, William Ross found a cat with folded ears in a **litter** of **domestic** cats. The cat was named Susie.

Later, Susie had a litter of kittens. Two of the kittens had folded ears. Ross and his wife Mary took one of the folded-ear kittens home. They named her Snooks. The Rosses **bred** Snooks, and the Scottish Fold breed began. Scottish Folds were registered in the United States in 1973, and gained championship status in 1978.

Scottish Fold cats are bred with American or British Shorthair cats with straight ears. Usually, about half of a litter will have the folded-ear **trait**. Scottish Fold cats with folded ears should never be bred together. Kittens that have two folded-ear parents often have abnormal **cartilage**. This can cause stiffness in joints such as the knee and tail.

All purebred Scottish Fold cats, such as this one, can trace their pedigree back to Susie.

Qualities

Scottish Folds are friendly cats. They are quiet, gentle, reserved, and intelligent. They can easily adapt to any living situation.

Scottish Folds are not easily upset. They get along well with children and other pets. They have a sweet, quiet voice. But you will not hear it often!

Scottish Fold cats are loving and friendly and do not demand attention. They will sit on your lap when you want them to. But they will not be bothered if you don't pay close attention to them. Scottish Folds do not need to be involved in what is going on around them. They will be fine if left alone for a day or two.

Scottish Folds are quiet and have soft voices.

Coat and Color

Scottish Fold cats can have short or long hair. The shorthaired Scottish Fold's coat is medium-short in length. The longhair **breed** has a medium-long coat. Both breeds' coats are plush, **dense**, and soft to touch. They come in every color except point-colors, such as Siamese colors.

A shorthaired Scottish Fold

Longhaired Scottish Folds are sometimes called Highland Folds.

Size

Scottish Folds are medium-sized cats. Their padded bodies are round and muscular. They are solid cats with long, tapering tails. Their legs are short to medium length. Often it appears that their legs are too short for their bodies!

Scottish Folds have rounded heads on short, thick necks. Their ears are rounded at the tip and lie on their heads like a cap.

Scottish Folds can have three kinds of folded ears. Slightly folded ears are called single fold. If the ears are folded about halfway, it is called double fold. Triple-fold ears lie flat against the head. This is the most desirable ear.

Some people think the Scottish Fold looks like an otter!

Care

Scottish Fold cats are quite easy to groom. They need to be brushed once a week with a medium-bristle brush. Longhaired cats may need to be groomed more often. Occasionally rubbing their coat with a **chamois** will bring out extra shine.

Like any cat, the Scottish Fold will frequently need to sharpen its claws. This is a natural behavior for all cats. Providing a scratching post for them to use will save your furniture from damage.

All cats love to play. Movement is important for their enjoyment. So try to provide them with toys they can move with their paws. A ball, **catnip** mouse, or anything they can move will be good.

Cats should be trained to use a **litter box**. The litter box needs to be cleaned every day. Cats should also be **spayed** or **neutered** unless you are planning on **breeding** them.

Longhaired Scottish Folds need to be brushed and combed twice a week.

Feeding

All cats are **carnivores**. They need food that is high in protein, such as meat or fish. Cats can be very picky and do not like changes in their diet.

Homemade diets usually do not provide the **nutrients** that cats need. A better choice is commercial cat food. It comes in three types. They are dry, semidry, and canned. Each kind offers similar nutritional value.

Dry foods are the most convenient. And they can prevent **tartar** buildup on your cat's teeth. Canned foods are the most appealing to cats. But they do not stay fresh for very long.

Because of their naturally padded body, it is important to watch how much Scottish Folds eat so they do not become overweight.

Cats also need fresh water every day. Your cat may love to drink milk. But many cats are unable to **digest** milk. It will often make them sick. Cats also love treats. You can find many treats at your local pet store.

Kittens

Baby cats are called kittens. The female cat is **pregnant** for about 65 days before the kittens are born. Scottish Folds usually have about five kittens in a **litter**. All are born with straight ears. Only about half will develop folded ears.

All kittens are born blind and helpless. They need to drink their mother's milk for the first three weeks. Then they start to eat solid food. Most kittens stop drinking their mother's milk when they are about eight weeks old.

Kittens start becoming independent when they are about three weeks old. By then they can see, hear, and stand on their own. At about seven weeks, they can run and play. When kittens are 12 weeks old, they can be sold or given away.

Kittens that have the folded-ear trait will develop folded ears when they are about four weeks old.

Buying a Kitten

A healthy cat will live about 14 to 16 years. A kitten becomes very attached to its owner. So before you buy a kitten, be sure you will be able to take care of it for as long as it lives.

There are many places to get kittens. A qualified **breeder** is the best place to buy a **purebred** kitten. When buying from a breeder, be sure to get the kitten's **pedigree** papers and health records. Pet shelters, veterinarians, and cat shows are also good places to find kittens.

When choosing a kitten, check to see that it is healthy. Its ears, nose, mouth, and fur should all be clean. The eyes should be bright and clear. The kitten should be alert and playful.

Glossary

breed - a group of cats that shares the same appearance and characteristics. A breeder is a person who raises cats. Raising cats is often called breeding them.

carnivore - a plant or animal that eats meat.

cartilage - the soft, elastic connective tissue in the skeleton. Your nose and ears are made of cartilage.

catnip - the dried leaves and stems of a plant in the mint family. Catnip is used as a stuffing in cat toys because some cats are attracted to its strong smell.

chamois - a soft, pliable leather or cloth.

dense - having many pieces in a small area.

digest - to break down food in the stomach.

domestic - animals that are tame.

Felidae - the Latin name for the cat family.

litter - all the kittens born at one time to a mother cat.

litter box - a box where cats dispose of their waste.

neuter - to remove a male animal's reproductive organs.

nutrients - vitamins and minerals that all living things need to survive.

pedigree - a record of an animal's ancestors.

pregnant - having one or more babies growing within the body.

purebred - an animal whose parents are both from the same breed.

spay - to remove a female animal's reproductive organs.

tartar - a crust that forms on the teeth. Tartar is made of saliva, food particles, and salt.

trait - a quality that distinguishes one person or group from another.

Web Sites

Would you like to learn more about Scottish Fold cats? Please visit **www.abdopub.com** to find up-to-date Web site links to more information on the Scottish Fold. These links are routinely monitored and updated to provide the most current information available.

Index